REYKJAVÍK REQUIEM

Gerður Kristný

REYKJAVÍK REQUIEM
S Á L U M E S S A

Translated by
Rory McTurk

with an Introduction by
Sigþrúður Gunnarsdóttir

2020

Published by Arc Publications
Nanholme Mill, Shaw Wood Road
Todmorden OL14 6DA, UK
www.arcpublications.co.uk

Copyright in original poems © Gerður Kristný 2020
Translation copyright © Rory McTurk 2020
Introduction copyright © Sigþrúður Gunnarsdóttir 2020
Copyright in this edition © Arc Publications 2020

Design and all photographs by Tony Ward
Printed in Great Britain by TJ International,
Padstow, Cornwall.

978 1 910345 01 6 (pbk)
978 1 910345 02 3 (ebk)

Sálumessa was originally published in 2018 by Forlagið
Publishing, Reykjavík, Iceland. The publishers are grateful
to Forlagið for their permission to reproduce the original
Icelandic text in this volume.

The information about untranslatable words is taken
from *Lost in Translation: An Illustrated Compendium of
Untranslatable Words* by Ella Frances Sanders
(London: Vintage Publishing, 2015)

This book is copyright. Subject to statutory exception and
to provisions of relevant collective licensing agreements, no
reproduction of any part, nor of the whole, may take place
without the written permission of Arc Publications Ltd.

This book has been translated with financial support from

Introduction

Reykjavík Requiem tells in powerful, succinct language the story of a woman who was abused as a child by her brother in a small Icelandic village. At the heart of the poem is the very notion of articulation, of how our language and culture determine what stories we can tell and what words we can use. The sections of the poem are interspersed with words found only in some languages and not in others, forming a refrain of which the essential message is that words fail us.

The woman who is the subject of the poem gave her own account of the affair, but committed suicide before it could appear in print. It was beyond her powers, in the words available to her, to break the silence about the violence she had suffered. Society was not in fact ready for stories of the kind she had to tell: the editor of the journal that published her story received the harshest criticism for doing so from the ethics committee of the Icelandic Association of Journalists. Some years later this editor was awarded a prize by that same Association for reporting another Icelandic woman's similar experience. The editor in question was Gerður Kristný, who later still found an outlet for her response in three powerful poetic sequences.

Reykjavík Requiem is closely related to the first two of these sequences, both published by Arc, and both portraying women who have been subjected to oppression and violence. These are *Bloodhoof,* in which Gerður rewrites the eddic poem *Skírnismál* from the point of view of her namesake, the giantess Gerður Gymisdóttir, whose view of its events differs altogether from that of the fertility god Freyr; and *Drápa: the Slaying – a Reykjavík Murder Mystery,* about the murder of a young woman in Reykjavík. In all three sequences Gerður employs trenchant and formal poetic language, conjuring up murky, bewildering images of the fates of women in which the cold and the dark are prominent and the boundaries between life and death, between our world and worlds that lie beyond, are unclear.

In all three sequences the speaking voice is at once compelling and mysterious. The speaker of *Reykjavík Requiem* seems to be some kind of being from the beyond, lying beside the dead woman in her grave, singing her requiem, and determined that her life should not be forgotten. The requiem recalls a musical composition beginning in slow, sluggish tones, which gradually rise to a crescendo before the work finally reaches a hushed conclusion once the earth that was wounded has reawakened at last.

The revolution enabling open discussion of sexual abuse and its results could only come about with a leap to loose the chains of thousands of years of suppression, allowing words to arise that could convey experience that was unbearable but needed to be acknowledged. Gerður Kristný is one of those writers who have played an active part in this revolution, with her repeated use of razor-sharp poetic language in saying what before could not be said, in endowing with a voice those who earlier had none, and in opening the eyes of those of us who were unaware of what words we needed and were lacking.

Sigþrúður Gunnarsdóttir

Author's Note

The reference on p. 52 to the murderess from Sjöundá is to Steinunn Sveinsdóttir from Sjöundá in western Iceland who, in the early nineteenth century, was sentenced to death for murdering her husband and for assisting her lover in the murder of his wife. She died in prison before the sentence could be carried out.

REYKJAVÍK REQUIEM

Grænlendingar eiga orð yfir að skima sífellt
eftir mannaferðum

I
K
T
S
U
A
R
P
O
K

The Greenlanders have a word for being constantly on
the lookout for passers-by

Lengi hef ég
dvalið með þér
í dysinni

heygð eins og
hundur með
eiganda sínum

Long have I
lain with you
in the burial-cairn

buried like
a dog
with its master

Höfuð í
landsuður

líkaminn í höm

Head laid
south-eastwards

with back to the wind

Innan seilingar:

Meitill
öngull
sigð

Við erum lík

Within reach:

Chisel
fish-hook
sickle

We are alike in death

Bærinn kvikur
af ljósum og leik

Beðið var
komu jólabarnsins

Förin
þegar hafin
yfir heiðina

Leiðin sópuð
með grenigreinum

        The town alive
        with lights and play

        Awaiting the coming
        of the Christmas child

        The journey
        across the heath
        already begun

        The way swept
        with Yule tree branches

Stjörnur
úr járni
lýstu upp stræti

Skíði ristu
hlíðar

Iron-wrought
stars
lit up the streets

Skis
slashed slopes

Pollurinn
lagður svelli

Það hvein
í ísnum undan
skautum barnanna

eins og
hníf væri
brugðið á brýni

The pond frozen
over with ice

An eery sound
arose in the ice
from beneath the children's skates

as of a knife
sharpened
on a whetstone

Hús þitt
hljótt og myrkt
sveipað
djúpum svefni

Your house
dark and silent
wrapped
in deep sleep

Grýlukerti uxu
fyrir glugga

Þú horfðir út um
vígtenntan skolt
vetrarins

Röddin drafandi
augnlokin rökkurþung

Icicles formed
at the window

You looked out through
the war-toothed jaw
of the winter

The voice muzzy
the eyelids dusk-heavy

Þú skrifaðir
sögu þína
blekvættum barrnálum

um bróður
sem lagði
líf þitt
pínu

You wrote
your story
with ink-moistened pine-needles

about a brother
who laid low
your life
with torment

Hann leitaði
á þig þegar
hann kenndi
þér að lesa

Ása sá sól
Ari rólar

Þú óttaðist að
það sama biði
barna hans

He touched you
overmuch
when teaching
you to read:

'Ása saw the sun'
'Ari takes a stroll'

You feared that the same
would befall
his children

Ekkert
heyrðist í þér
í þorpinu þar sem
varnargarðurinn
beit af sér brimið
en veitti þér
aldrei skjól

No sound
was heard from you
in the village where
the protective wall
fended off breakers
but never granted you
shelter

Bernska þín
botnfrosin tjörn

Nú hafðirðu
mulið utan
af þér ísinn

hrist af þér
hrönglið

Enginn
skyldi þola
það sama
og þú

Your childhood a lake
frozen to its depths

By now you had
crushed off
the ice around you

shaken off
its frail hold

No-one
was to suffer
the same
as you

Oft hafðirðu
reynt að
flýta fyrir þér

Nú sastu þarna
umlukin eigin myrkri

Often
had you tried
to make a swift end of it

You sat there surrounded
by your own darkness

Bringan
bærðist ekki

andardrátturinn
ógreinilegur

The breast
motionless

the breath
faint

Úti
kölluðust
krakkar á

Það rofaði til
í svefninum

Outside
were children
calling to each other

Clouds cleared
in your sleep

Börn!

Það besta
sem þú vissir!

Eitt andartak
sást hver þú
hefðir getað orðið

Children!

The best thing
you knew!

For one moment
it was clear
who you could have been

Í farsi finnst orð yfir ljómann í augum okkar
þegar við eignumst vin

Það vantar orð yfir skelfinguna sem hríslast eins og
snjóbráð niður eftir hryggnum

T
I
Á
M

There's a word in Farsi for the gleam in our eyes when
we make a new friend

There's no word for the terror which trickles like melting
snow down your back

Heiðlóa á haugi
vekur upp draug

Mild er moldin
feldur sem heldur
á okkur hita

Ég seilist
í sigðina
vek mér blóð

læk sem lekur
til þín

        On the mound a golden plover
        calls a ghost from the grave

        Soft is the earth
        as a furred cloak holding
        the heat within us

        I reach out
        for the sickle
        let the blood run free

        a streamlet leaking
        in your direction

Taumurinn
tengir okkur

konur
huslaðar í holti

The streak of blood linking
the two of us

women
unhouseled in a hillock

Kræki
úr mér auga
með öngli

leik með það
í lófa

I gouge out
an eye of mine
with the hook

play with it
in the palm of my hand

Enn sefurðu
svefninum stranga

Auga mitt
dapurt af harmi
gefur þér gætur

You continue to sleep
the last long sleep

That eye of mine
stricken with sorrow
watches over you

Ég sting því
aftur í tóttina

læt lítið
fyrir mér fara

Þungt dynur
þögnin í
moldinni

I replace it
in its socket

make myself
fade from view

The silence falls
with a thud
in the earth

Þú varst ein
þegar svertan
í augunum
breiddist yfir blámann

Ása á
ól

You were alone
when the blackness
in your eyes
overspread the blue

'Ása has
a leather strap'

Háðir dóm
yfir heimi
sem aldrei
hélt skildi yfir þér

Sagðir þig
úr lögum
við lífið
sofnaðir svefni
hinna dauðu

You passed judgement
on a world
which shielded you
never

You resigned
from the laws
of life
slept the sleep
of the dead

Þótt hjartað
hætti að slá
starfar heilinn
um stund

Leiftra um
lög hugans:

Sorg
Fegurð
Fögnuður

Though the heart
ceases to beat
the brain works
for a time

Round the layers
of the mind flash:

Sorrow
Beauty
Joy

Þú hvarfst
inn í vetrarríkið

jörðinni
og steinunum
og trjánum
og öllum málmum

You vanished away
into winter's kingdom

from the earth
and from the stones
and from the trees
and all metals

Handan við suður
ofan við norður

stefndir í dauður

Beyond southwards
above northwards

you headed deathwards

Lést heiminum eftir
glænýja höfuðátt

og loforð um
að láta nafn þitt
aldrei uppi

Bequeathing to the world
a fifth compass point

and a promise never
to let your name
be told

Í wagiman-málinu er til orð yfir að leita í vatni
með fótunum

Það vantar orð yfir tímann sem það tekur harm
að hjaðna

M
U
R
R

M
A

In the Wagiman language there is a word for
searching in the water with only your feet

There is no word for the time it takes for sorrow
to subside

Undir
sorgarfargi
djúp gjóta

gengur
sundur og saman
bryður liði
og bein

skoltur
á mannýgu dýri

Beneath
the weight of sorrow
a deep cavity

clicks apart
and together
crunches joints
and bones

the jaw
of a killing beast

Nóttin kveikti
á kolu sinni

Dysin
gránuð skímu

The night lit
its lantern

The burial-cairn
now grey in faint light

Einn steinn
frá hverjum þeim
sem fór hjá

Hey undir
höfði

Beinin máð
af þukli

One stone
from each person
who passed by

Hay beneath
the head

The bones worn away
by fingering

Helvíti, hér er sigur þinn

Dauði, hér er broddur þinn

Hell, here is thy victory

Death, here is thy sting

Nafn þitt
næðir um
huga minn

liðast
niður í munn

tefst á tungu
bráðnar á broddi

Sleppur
aldrei út

Your name
sends a cold wind
round my mind

falls in waves
into my mouth

is detained on my tongue
dissolves on its tip

And never
escapes

Það er dýrt
að vera dáin

Steinunn á Sjöundá
skuldaði leigu

landskuld

ljóstoll

It is costly
to be dead

The murderess from Sjöundá
owed rent

land-rent

lighting tax

Fólkið þitt
var dapurt

það vildi
launin þín
það síðasta sem
þú vannst þér inn

Your people
were downcast

They wanted
your money
your very
last earnings

Það er
dýrt að jarða,
sagði það

Þú skyldir sjálf
kaupa þér kistu

Nafn bróður þíns
undir dánartilkynningunni

Burials are
expensive
they said

You were to buy
your own coffin

Your brother's name appearing
under your death announcement

Fólkið vildi ekki
að sagan bærist út

Hún vatt sér
undir augnlok þeirra
sleit þau af
sem blöð af blómi

Enginn unni
sér hvíldar

They didn't want the story
to get around

It moved swiftly
beneath their eyelids
tore them off
like petals from a flower

No-one
found rest

Þau þyrluðu þögn
yfir orð þín
örfínu lagi af lygum
svo enginn þyrði
að hafa þau eftir

They swirled silence
over your words
an intricate layer of lies
so that no-one would dare
to repeat them

Seinna skilaði
fólkið þitt
laununum
– klinki í plastpoka

30 silfurpeningar!
sagði það

Your people later
paid back
the money
– loose change in a plastic bag

30 pieces of silver!
they said

Vissulega varstu
mannsdóttirin
sem var fórnað

Sagan þín
birtist svo hver
sem á hana trúir
glatist ekki

You were indeed
the daughter of man
she who was sacrificed

Your story
is made known
so that each who believes in it
will not be lost

Hyllið dótturina,
þið dómarar
á jörðu!

Kiss the daughter
ye judges
of the earth!

Launin runnu
til kvenna
sem þolað
höfðu pínu
líkt og þú

Vonandi
keyptu þær sér
dulu að dansa í

The money found its way
to women
who had suffered
torment
as you had

Let us hope
they each bought
a shroud to dance in

Lífið reisti þér
myrkurkirkju
hvar þú máttir
næðis njóta
– nafnlausa
fórnarbarn –

úr rekaviði
sokknum skipum

Life built for you
a church of darkness
where you could enjoy
peace and quiet
– thou nameless
sacrificial child –

built it from driftwood
from sunken ships

Bekkir úr
ekka

Bláir fingur
fálma eftir
sálmabók

Pews made from
keening

Blue fingers
fumbling
for a hymnbook

Andköf
stíga úr kórnum

Hundruð hausa
syngja þér
sálumessu

stjaksettir strjúpar

Gasps for breath
ascending from the choir

Hundreds of heads
singing your
requiem

with necks pole-impaled

Finnar eiga orð yfir vegalengdina sem hreindýr
ferðast án hvíldar

Það vantar orð yfir kuldann sem nístir okkur þegar
vinir velja að deyja

P
O
R
U
N
K
U
S
E
M
A

The Finns have a word for the distance the reindeer
travel without resting

There is no word for the cold that chills us when
friends choose to die

Vakna í
ærandi birtu

Bælið þitt
er autt!

Haugurinn rofinn!

I awake
in blinding light

Your resting place
is empty!

The burial-mound broken open!

Þú hefur verið
numin á brott

Tíminn
storknaður taumur
á moldargólfi

You have been
snatched away

Time now a streak
of congealed blood
on a floor of earth

Nú hvílir þú
í helgri jörð
mýkri og dýpri
en sú sem við deildum

Vetrarríkið
verndi þig
og gæti

Now you are resting
in holy ground
softer and deeper
than that which we shared

May winter's kingdom
protect you
and guard you

Ég tek fram
öngulinn
og rimpa saman
á mér varirnar

I take hold
of the fish-hook
and cobble together
my lips

Kem mér
upp úr kumlinu

munda meitil
hegg bát
úr hamri

Heave myself
from the howe

aim the chisel
hew a boat
from the cliff

Bálast upp
reiði mín!

Bróður þinn
dæmi ég til
sjógangs

fleyti mannlausum
steinnökkva
að finna hann
tyrfðan
blóðvættum barrnálum

My wrath
is kindled!

I condemn
your brother
to the open sea

I set afloat
a crewless stone ship
to find him
turfed over
with blood-moistened pine-needles

Hann þræðir firði
slæðir hafnir
grýttum kili

Það hriktir
í þóftu

Nú eru lyktir
í nánd

It threads its way
through fjords, dredges harbours
with stony keel

The thwart
is creaking

Now the end
is at hand

Ég stefni
bróður þínum
um borð

Sviptur áttum
og svefni
leggur hann
á reginhaf

I summon
your brother
on board

Stripped of bearings
and sleep
he sets out
on the raging sea

inn í sömu
stjarnlausu nóttina
og dró þig
inn í dauðann

into the same
starless night
as dragged you
into death

Svo gliðnar grjótið

Raðir
hvassra keipa
vaxa upp úr
borðstokknum

The ship's stones slip and slide

Rows
of sharp rowlocks
sprout from
the gunwale

Bátskjafturinn
hvolfist yfir hann

keiparnir
ganga inn í
bringu og hrygg

Rökkurnökkvinn
sekkur

The ship's mouth
encloses him

The rowlocks
enter his
breast and backbone

The twilight ship
sinks

Í urdu er til orð um gleðina yfir að einhver elski
okkur af öllu hjarta

Það vantar orð yfir kvíðann þegar við óttumst að fenni
yfir minningarnar

N
A
Z

In Urdu there's a word for the joy we feel when someone
loves us with their whole heart

There is no word for the anxiety we feel when we fear
that memories will be snowed under

Um huga
ástvina þinna
eigrar óljós minning
um stúlku

Through the minds
of your dear ones
drifts the faint memory
of a girl

Hún horfir
í gegnum
íshelluna
sem bróðirinn
steypti henni

Nývöknuð
inn í draum
sem hún velur
hvernig endar

She gazes
through the floe
of ice
which her brother
moulded for her

Newly awakened
into a dream
of which she chooses
the end

Síðan hefur
ekkert verið samt

Klakinn bráðnar
vakir opnast

Tjarnir
fljóta yfir
bakka sína

Since then nothing
has been the same

The ice melts
with holes opening up

Lakes
overflow
their banks

Hörkur
hafa tekið við

myrkur læsist
um landið

Harsh weather
has taken charge
darkness
engulfs the land

Vígahnöttur
á vetrarhimni

slóðinn
slægir dökkvann

A meteor
in a winter sky

its track
disembowels the darkness

Þíða leggst
yfir landið

Þó marar
klaki úti
í ánni

hvítar
hvassyddaðar
raðir

A thaw
comes over the land

Yet the ice
floats half-submerged
in the river

in white
sharp-pointed
rows

Tennurnar
hafa verið
dregnar úr
vetrinum

The teeth
have been
extracted
from the winter

Hjarnið
hrúður á særðri jörð

hún ber
sitt barr

The snowcrust a scab
on the wounded earth

which shows signs
of healing

Gleymir mér
heimur

Daprast mér
draumar

The world
forgets me

I dream
no longer

Það vantar orð yfir snjóinn sem sest á örgranna
grein bjarkar í stingandi stillu

There's no word for the snow which settles on the
slimmest of birch-limbs in pin-pricking calm

Það vantar orð

There's no word

Icelandic Pronunciation:
an approximate guide

In this bilingual edition of *Sálumessa*, readers are strongly advised to compare the translation with the original Icelandic. Those readers who know Icelandic will soon find that the translation is not a literal one, and cannot always be matched word for word with the original. But whether they know Icelandic or not, readers will gain much from reading the poem aloud in the original language. With this in mind I give below a brief approximate guide to Icelandic pronunciation, covering only those points that are relevant to a reading of *Sálumessa*. It makes no claim to overall coverage, and the lists of examples given are not claimed to be exhaustive.

NB: The stress should always be on the first syllable of the word.

Vowels without acute accents over them are pronounced very much as in English, except that:

a falls somewhere between the standard English pronunciations of *father* and *fat*

a followed by *ng* (as in e.g. *stranga*, p. 36, *ganga*, p. 77) is pronounced like *ow* in English *how*

i and *y* are pronounced as in English *hit*

i followed by *ng* (as in *sting*, p. 37, *syngja*, p. 63) is

95

pronounced like *ee* in *seen* (for the pronunciations of *g* and *j*, see below)

 u is pronounced as in *put* (not as in *but*)
 æ is pronounced like English *eye*
 ö like *oe* in *Goethe*
 The diphthong *au* is pronounced like *eui* in French *feuille* (not like *au* in German *Haus*),
 The diphthongs *ei* and *ey* are pronounced like *ay* in English *day*

Vowels with acute accents are pronounced as follows:
á like English *ow* in *how*
é like *ye* in *yes*
í and *ý* like *ee* in *seen*
ó like English *oh*
ú like *oo* in *moon*

As for the consonants, the two letters least familiar to novices, *þ* and *ð*, are pronounced as follows:
þ like *th* in English *thin*
ð like *th* in English *that*
The consonants *b*, *d*, *h*, *k*, *m*, *t*, *v*, and single *l*, *m*, and *n* are pronounced much as in English.

f is pronounced:
(1) like *f* in English *father* at the beginning of a word (*Förin*, p. 17) or word-element (*botnfrosin*, p. 25) and before *t* (*aftur*, p. 37) or *s* (*hvarfst*, p. 41, *tefst*, p. 51)
(2) like English *p* before *n* (*svefni*, pp. 20, 74, *sofnaðir*

svefni, p. 39, *svefninum*, pp. 28, 36, *nafn*, pp. 43, 51, 54, *nafnlausa* (with *n* after *f* all but lost to the ear), p. 61, *hafnir*, p. 73, *stefni*, p. 74), except that (3) it is all but lost if followed by *nd* (*stefndir*, p. 42) (4) otherwise, like English *v* in the middle or the end of a word (*Höfuð*, p. 14, *hafin*, p. 17, *horfðir, drafandi*, p. 21)

g (never pronounced as in English *George* or *engine*) is pronounced:
(1) like English *g* (as in *green, glow, gash, get, guide*, etc.) at the beginning of a word or word-element (*Grænlendingar*, p. 11, *grenigreinum*, p. 17, *glugga*, p. 21, *varnargarðurinn*, p. 24, *getað*, p. 29, *gefur þér gætur*, p. 36, *glænýja*, p. 43, *gæti*, p. 69)
(2) after *n* as in English *anger, linger, hunger* (not as in *hanging, singing, hung*) (*Lengi*, p. 13, *öngull*, p. 15, *Enginn*, pp. 25, 55, 56, *tengir*, p. 34, *stranga*, p. 36, *tungu*, p. 51, *fingur*, p. 62, *syngja*, p. 63, *ganga, bringu*, p. 77), except when the combination *ng* occurs before a consonant (other than *j*), in which case the *g* is less strongly pronounced (*hrönglið*, p. 25, *öngli*, p. 35) or all but lost to the ear (*Þungt*, p. 37, *sjógangs*, p. 72)
(3) like *g* in Spanish *luego* when it occurs singly after a vowel or after *au* or *ei*, whether at the end of a word or immediately followed by *a* or *u* (*ég, og*, p. 13, *eiga*, pp. 11, 65, *eiganda*, p. 13, *þegar*, p. 17, *sögu*, p. 22, *draug*, p. 33, *auga*, pp. 35, 36, *augunum*, p. 38, *lögum*, p. 39, *lög hugans*, p. 40, *mannýgu*, p. 47, *huga*, pp. 51, 81, *lygum*, p.

56, *Haugurinn*, p. 67)

(4) also like *g* in Spanish *luego* when it occurs singly after a vowel or after *ey* or *ei* and precedes *ð* or *r* (*heygð*, p. 13, *lagður*, *brugðið*, p. 19, *Sagðir*, p. 39, *sagði*, pp. 54, 57, *sigðina*, p. 33, *eigrar*, p. 81)

(5) like *y* in *yes* when it occurs singly after a vowel or after *au*, *ei*, or *æ* and is immediately followed by *i* (*eigin*, p. 26, *haugi*, p. 33, *lagi*, p. 56, *reginhaf*, p. 74, *slægir*, p. 85)

(6) otherwise in general much like English *g* (*pögnin*, p. 37, *Sorg*, *Fögnuður*, p. 40, *sorgarfargi*, p. 47, *þögn*, p. 56, *helgri*, p. 69), except that in the consonant clusters in *augnlokin*, p. 21 and *augnlok*, p. 55, the *g* is almost lost to the ear.

gg is pronounced as in English, though somewhat more emphatically (*hegg*, p. 71, *leggur*, p. 74, *hrygg*, p. 77)

hv may be pronounced either as *kv* (as in *akvavit*), or with full value given to the *h* and the *v* as each of these two letters is pronounced in English (*hvein*, p. 19, *hver*, pp. 29, 58, *hvarfst*, p. 41, *hvíldar*, pp. 55, 65, *hvolfist*, p. 77, *einhver*, p. 79, *hvítar hvassyddaðar*, p. 86)

j is pronounced like English *y* in *yes*

ll is pronounced like *ttl* in settler, e.g. *Meitill*, *öngull*, p. 15, *Pollurinn*, *svelli*, p. 19, *kölluðust*, p. 28, *öllum*, p. 41, *ljóstoll*, p. 52, *hyllið*, p. 59, *íshelluna*, p. 82, *stillu*, p. 91, except that in the case of *sífellt*, pp. 11, it is pronounced like English *guilty* with the tip of the tongue raised to the back of the upper front teeth

mm is pronounced as in English, though with the sound somewhat protracted

nn is also pronounced much as in English, except that when following *ei* (as in *Einn steinn*, p. 49, *Seinna*, p. 57) it sounds like *tn* in *Etna* (in the case of *steinnökkva*, p. 72, however, where *nn* joins two word-elements, it is pronounced as in English, though with the sound somewhat protracted)

p is pronounced as in English, though not before before *t*, where it is pronounced like *f* (1), above (*keyptu* p. 60, *sviptur*, p. 74, *steypti*, p. 82)

r is more strongly trilled than in English, so that *rn* sounds somewhat like *tn* (*Stjörnur úr járni*, p. 18, *varnargarðurinn*, p. 24, *fórnarbarn*, p. 61, *varirnar*, p. 70, *Tjarnir*, p. 83, *Tennurnar*, p. 87)

s should be pronounced as in *house*, not as in *rose*.

Rory McTurk

Biographical Notes

GERÐUR KRISTNÝ was born in 1970 and brought up in Reykjavík and graduated in French and Comparative Literature from the University of Iceland in 1992. She is now a full-time writer.

Gerður Kristný has published poetry, short stories, novels and books for children, and a biography *Myndin af pabba – Saga Thelmu* (A Portrait of Dad – Thelma's Story) for which she won the Icelandic Journalism Award in 2005.

Other awards for her work include the Children's Choice Book Prize in 2003 for *Marta Smarta* (Smart Martha), the Halldór Laxness Literary Award in 2004 for her novel *Bátur með segli og allt* (A Boat with Sail and All) and the West-Nordic Children's Literature Prize in 2010 for the novel *Garðurinn* (The Garden).

Three of her poetry collections, *Höggstaður* (Soft Spot), *Blóðhófnir* (Bloodhoof) and *Sálumessa* (Requiem) have been nominated for the Icelandic Literature Prize, with *Blóðhófnir* winning the prize in 2014. *Bloodhoof* and *Drápa (The Slaying)*, translated into English by Rory McTurk, were published in bilingual editions by Arc in 2012 and 2018 respectively, and publication of this book completes the trilogy.

Gerður Kristný lives in Reykjavík but travels regularly around the world to present her work.

Rory McTurk graduated from Oxford in 1963, took a further degree at the University of Iceland, Reykjavík in 1965, and after teaching at the universities of Lund and Copenhagen, and then University College, Dublin, took up a post at Leeds University in 1978.

In addition to his two authored books, *Studies in Ragnars Saga Loðbrókar and its Major Scandinavian Analogues* (Oxford, 1991) and *Chaucer and the Norse and Celtic Worlds* (Aldershot, 2005), he has edited the *Blackwell Companion to Old Norse-Icelandic Literature and Culture* (Oxford, 2004), and co-edited, with Andrew Wawn, a volume of essays, *Úr Dölum til Dala* (From Dalir to the Dales) (Leeds, 1989) in commemoration of the Icelandic scholar Guðbrandur Vigfússon (1827-89). He has contributed editions of Old Norse works of literature to *A New Introduction to Old Norse, Part II, Reader*, 5th edition, ed. Anthony Faulkes (London, 2011) and to *Skaldic Poetry of the Scandinavian Middle Ages*, Vol. VIII, ed. Margaret Clunies Ross (Turnhout, 2017).

His publications also include two Icelandic saga translations, two book-length translations of scholarly works on Icelandic topics (one from Swedish, the other from Icelandic), numerous essays and articles, and translations (published in 2007 and 2015) of two novels by the Icelandic writer Steinunn Sigurðardóttir: *Tímaþjófurinn* (The Thief of Time) (Reykjavík, 1986) and *jójó* (Yo-yo) (Reykjavík, 2011).

His translations of Gerður Kristný's *Blóðhófnir* (Bloodhoof, Reykjavík, 2010) and *Drápa* (The Slaying, Reykjavík, 2014) were published by Arc in 2012 and 2018.